IN THE LAND OF MOAB

IN THE LAND OF MOAB

photographs of a canyon wilderness

Photographs & Essays by Tom Till

FABLE VALLEY PUBLISHERS, INC.

INTERNATIONAL STANDARD BOOK NUMBER
0-9712555-0-4

LIBRARY OF CONGRESS NUMBER
2001094137

Published by
Fable Valley Publishers, Inc.
P.O. Box 337
Moab, Utah 84532
435-259-5327

Printed in China by Everbest Printing

BOOK PRODUCTION NOTES

Design by Michael Snell, Shade of the Cottonwood, LLC
Computer, scanning and production consultant, Duncan Mackie
Scans by Clay Schwarck
Production assistance by Marcy Till, Ann Carter, Eve Tallman
Labwork by John Botkin, Photocraft, Inc.
Field logistics by Glen Lathrop
Photographic adviser, Steve Mulligan

From original 4x5 transparencies, scans were created using an Imacon Flextight
Precision II Scanner and a Macintosh G4 with Photoshop. Hard proofs were
done on an Epson Printer. Scans were transmitted overseas on CDs burned
on a Yamaha CDRW.

ACKNOWLEDGEMENTS

Thanks to my family, Marcy, Mikenna, and Bryce. Thanks especially to my wife
who encouraged me to pursue this project. I extend my deepest gratitude to
the many people I've shared outdoors experiences with over years in the Moab
area. Many thanks to Glen Van Nimwegen, fellow Iowan, and photographer
extraordinaire, for showing me his 4x5 transparencies in 1976. The beauty of
his work still inspires me and has had a profound effect on my life.

Cover photograph:
Park Avenue in Fog, Arches National Park
Back cover photograph:
La Sal Mountains and Castle Rock, proposed La Sal Waters Wilderness

Visit the Tom Till Gallery
61 North Main, Moab, Utah 84532
435-259-9808 or 888-479-9808
www.tomtill.com

CONTENTS

FOREWORD:

I WAS A CANYONLANDS PRODIGY. Some of my first memories involved intently studying the landscape revealed in the *Arizona Highways* magazines my grandmother and mother diligently collected. These images got into my head like an unforgettable melody. Publisher Gibbs Smith wrote in the wonderful book *Blessed by Light,* "The Colorado Plateau selects its people. If chosen you know: this landscape speaks to your emotions and spirit." I'm one of those. Though I seem to have an insatiable love for natural landscapes of all types, Moab is my home—it's where I was meant to be. I never tire of just looking around and drinking it all in.

When I was perhaps six, I saw an image of Delicate Arch and the La Sal Mountains in the natural history book, *The World We Live In.* As I looked at the flat, tamed Midwestern landscape out my window, I struggled to comprehend how such a thing as a rock arch could exist. It seemed as fantastic as the old black and white Flash Gordon serials on TV, and yet the arch was real.

After spending my college years dreaming about the West and Moab, I moved permanently from Iowa to the canyonlands in 1975. I'd picked a boom time in Grand County, and, even though I advertised in the local paper for a place to live for an entire summer, I received no calls. Finally, I spent my life savings from playing in rock and roll bands to buy a tiny trailer, parking it on one of the few available spaces in a dusty park in Spanish Valley. One week later, like an addict given pure heroin, I had climbed Mount Mellenthin, jeeped around the White Rim, and hiked to the Dark Angel. It was one of the most joyful periods of my life.

Since that time, my explorations have taken me to every corner of the Canyonlands, and I'm lucky enough to hike, search, dream, and create for a living. A few of the images here are unpublished work from the very beginnings of my 4x5 work in 1978-80. Also included is the first photograph I ever published, which had not appeared in book form before. Other photographs here include the most popular prints from the Tom Till Gallery, and the majority come from 1997 to the present, including many from 2001.

The desert isn't so solitaire anymore. Recreational use of the rivers, canyons, mesas, and mountains seems out of control and destined to threaten the very bedrock of the landscape. Development and sprawl continue apace, including mega resorts that will change the soul of our ramshackle valley forever. Every week brings a new meeting, or new decisions with profound repercussions for Moab and the land that surrounds us. A satellite map in the July, 2001 issue of *National Geographic Magazine* reveals the Moab Valley as a place of moderate urban sprawl, confirming the fears of many residents concerned about the burgeoning growth of Moab since 1990.

My goal with this portfolio, as always, is to ask for an appraisal of the beauty that still surrounds us. To protect what

> The desert isn't so solitaire anymore.

still exists from crowds, images herein that come from lesser known and fragile areas are captioned merely by subject and not location. I have also whittled down the number of archaeological images to a very few, to protect these especially fragile places.

A very hopeful turn of events is the work done in recent years by a number of local, regional and national environmental groups. Every Moab resident and visitor owes these groups a debt of thanks. They include The Nature Conservancy, The Glen Canyon Group of the Sierra Club, Living Rivers/Glen Canyon Action Group, the Southern Utah Wilderness Alliance, The Utah Open Lands Trust, The Castle Rock Collaboration and Redrock Forests. Passage of the Citizen's Red Rock Wilderness Bill now pending in Congress would go a long way toward preserving many of the areas pictured in this portfolio. In 2000, one third of the after tax profits of the Tom Till Gallery went to these groups and other charitable organizations.

I thought long and hard before I decided to go through with this project, because I do not want to bring more crowds to our doorstep. But, I do think I have something important to communicate. Compared to the number of people who would see one national car ad that promotes Moab as a "cool place," only a tiny number of people will see the pictures in this book. Even so, I worry my work will have some negative unintended effect. I weigh that concern against the heartfelt, trendless, and pure passion I feel for this land, and the natural desire I have to express my feeling with others.

I believe the highest and best use of the Canyon Country is contemplation. Here is beauty, mystery, knowledge, and wilderness on an almost infinite scale. We've lost something pure and integral when we see the rivers, canyons, mesas, and mountains only as backdrops for fun.

"In the desert
that faces Moab
toward
the sunrise."

—Numbers 21:13

MOAB VALLEY

RIVERS

PLATE 1

"S" Curve in Green River
Proposed BLM Wilderness

Light My Tire

THE COLORADO RIVER was the stern school marm of my youth. As a young river runner, I had nightmares after some trips, haunted by high water and Scylla and Charybdis dangers, but mostly, I used the river instead of a backpack to get my camera gear into the wilderness. The current did all the work. I liked the rapids okay, but they were really just obstacles keeping me from the next beautiful and photogenic side canyon. Also, river trips were a way for close friends to travel in the canyons together. In our boats with silly names like the "Death Cheater" and the "E. Ruess," and our childlike pirate games, we blew off steam from our jobs as teachers, publishers, professors, and geologists.

Attending the many meetings on the Canyonlands River Management Plan led me to a chance encounter with Gordon Topham, then Superintendent of Dead Horse Point State Park. Since the State of Utah claims jurisdiction over waterways in Utah, Topham was keen to hire a summer ranger to enforce state law on the "daily" section of the Colorado, extending roughly from Dewey downstream to Moab. My high school teaching job paid only $12,000 per year, and I was happy to pick up any job to keep me in film during the summer months.

Over the next several years, my duties provided me with a number of interesting moments. I saw one boatman, in a heated dispute, smack another with an oar, sending him to the hospital. I watched an eerie, unmanned boat ply its way down the river (after flipping on the Dolores River, the boat had flipped upright again, continuing on down river sans passengers), and I was once attacked by a group of drunken Moabites when I calmly suggested their children might be better off in Ken's Lake with life jackets. Although my job charged me with maintaining public safety, and I worried I would be blamed for any deaths on my watch, I personally believed that people who wanted to kill themselves on the Colorado River, or Ken's Lake, should be allowed to do so. Innocent children did not fall into this category.

During one slow, late season spell, I was given permission to spend several days on a series of river cleanup trips. In particular, I wanted to cleanse the small sandbar we called Tire Island, just downstream from Dewey. Somewhere upstream, an odious tire business had long been dumping its flotsam into the River, which then, due to its capricious currents, would drop Firestones and Goodyears on the shoals of sad Tire Island. Surrounded by the Colorado's flow, the atoll was accessible only by boat. The project seemed like a natural—clean up the eyesore, get some good exercise, and escape from the daily grind of checking life jackets and boatman's licenses. To help me, I enlisted my friend Tom Strawman, now a literature professor in Tennessee, and Karla Vanderzanden, then a BLM ranger and now director of Canyonlands Field Institute.

Releasing the entombed tires was much more like mud wrestling and greased pig grappling than we realized, and we became more encrusted in thick stinky mud each time we hoisted another tire into my 18' Havasu raft. The only pleasant part of the task was the cool insulation the mud gave us from the sweltering August temperatures. We continued the process for several days, bringing nearly 50 tires up to the Moab garbage dump each time. At last, late in the week, the slime belched up one more tire, covered with primordial mud as shiny black as any raven's wings. After a celebratory drive past the now-immaculate island, we returned to Moab for one last trip to the dump, and after a shower, a toast to our success.

I lived just below the Moab dump in those days, and though it was later celebrated by Moab boosters in the mid'80s as "The World's Most Scenic Dump," the Grand County landfill was sometimes a smoking wound, filling the valley with second-hand smoke of the worst kind. As I awoke the next morning, the pall was worse than ever, as thick clouds of dark smoke eclipsed the sun and enshrouded the entire valley. My tires were burning! My big cleanup, my environmental good deed, my aesthetic triumph, had filled the entire space between the La Sal Mountains and Arches National Park with a toxic cloud.

In the twenty years since, Tire Island has remained Michelin-free and the Moab dump no longer burns, but I think of the tires often. Are my images the same? Are they helping or hurting? Is every photograph a double-edged sword, working to preserve and working to endanger?

> I saw one boatman,
> in a heated dispute,
> smack another with
> an oar...

PLATE 2

Pictographs

....

PLATE 3

Flood Run Off Turning Colorado River Orange

PLATE 6

Fisher Towers and Colorado River

··

PLATE 7

Dead Horse Point State Park

PLATE 10

Waterfall into Colorado River

....

PLATE 11

Buttermilk Clouds
Colorado River

MESAS

PLATE 12

Wilson Arch and Single-Leaf Ash

Dear Abbey

I MOVED TO MOAB IN 1975 with no job prospects. All my attempts at getting a teaching job at Grand County High School had failed, as had my search for any other gainful employment. Fortunately, I was young and unlike many local job seekers, I had a college degree with some graduate study. This educational background helped me obtain my first job in Moab—breaking rocks in the hot sun.

Then Mayor Harold Jacobs hired me for a government makework scheme building flood check dams above the Walker Subdivision area of town. Subject to violent flash flooding from the solid rock which is now the Slickrock Bike Trail, this part of Moab needed protection from nature's furies, and my cohorts—college students on summer breaks and other gainfully unemployed townspeople—were there to help. It was August, it was feverishly hot, and it was a job. Our main task was breaking big rocks into little ones, drudgery broken only by the occasional rock behemoth that required dynamite. While the blast was readied and consummated, we hid in the shade. Besides lunch and a furtive cloud now and then, it was our only break from the anvil of the sun.

Fortunately, after about a month of dam construction, I landed a second job as station manager for Sun Valley Key Airlines at Canyonlands Field. Key Airlines, as it was later called, was one of the series of carriers who've tried to make a go of air service to and from Moab. Though all have been aided by subsidies from the federal government, the low passenger loads and the difficulty of booking seats has seen numerous airlines come and go in the last

25 years. I loved the job. I was radio operator, travel agent, ticket agent, baggage handler, freight delivery man, and weather observer. The part I particularly loved was observing the weather. Hourly, I looked to the sky and determined the type of clouds, the cloud cover percentage, and ascertained if any precipitation was falling, and of what kind and intensity. Temperature, wind, and dewpoint were also important. Lives depended on my "obs," so I took the job very seriously although shining the floodlight up to check the cloud ceiling at night, or sending up balloons during the day was just good, clean fun. Today, a computerized machine does all this, but not with the poetic flair ("dark, lowering clouds on Tavaputs Plateau, north") that I did.

My test came with the first big, and early, winter storm of the season on October 17, 1975. All the flights were canceled except the "bank" flight that landed in dozens of small Wyoming, Idaho, and Utah towns carrying canceled checks. The plane that day carried just one passenger, and I made observations every 15 minutes to help them get into the snowbound airport. Outside, as I checked the instruments, wet sage had saturated the air with a wonderful, medicinal aroma. The clouds were dark, cerulean blue, and the heavy moisture-laden snow had flocked every pinyon and juniper. Traffic on Highway 191, then called 163, ceased. I've loved every winter storm since then, and kept a mental catalog of them. Fortunately, the bank run landed safely, and although the passenger

> Lives depended on my "obs" so I took the job very seriously...

was very airsick he continued to Blanding. I didn't envy him, as the pilot was walking unsteadily himself.

Another red letter event occurred the next day. Each morning I received a list of passengers with reservations. These customers did not have to buy tickets, but merely express their supposed desire to travel to Salt Lake City to obtain a reservation, and only about one in four passengers actually showed up for a flight.

During the course of my job, I had met many of Moab's elite: Sam Taylor, Ken McDougald (namesake of Ken's Lake), Charlie Steen (the uranium king), and others, but that morning, the list contained a magical name for me— "Abbey, E."

The obsessive/compulsive nature which has helped me persevere with my photographic work has also made me, at times, a serious fan. During my life that fan energy has been directed at everything from Stanley Kubrick movies and Walt Whitman poetry to Seinfeld and Brian Wilson. Like an army of other people I had loved Abbey's work since I was assigned to read *Desert Solitaire* in college, and his writing was beginning to appear in all the magazines I read like *Backpacker, Wilderness* and *Sierra*. Often, the writing was teamed with images of the West and Canyon Country, and since photography was a burgeoning interest of mine, I became an even bigger fan.

Hoping to get my copy of the canyon country classic *Slickrock* signed by Cactus Ed, I rushed back to my trailer in

Moab, grabbed the coffeetable volume and and waited patiently behind my desk in my '70s sport jacket for the great man to arrive. Though my attention was torn away slightly by checking in passengers and luggage for the trip, I waited nervously, scanning the old Canyonlands Field Airport building for my reclusive, bearded hero. Soon, departure time came and went , with no sign of Abbey. Feeling a little foolish, I watched the plane depart in the darkness. Mr. Abbey had stood me up.

Over the next few months, this situation repeated itself at least a half dozen times. Ed was oviously somebody who made airline reservations and did not keep them. I never learned why. Perhaps he had been forced to leave Moab for whatever reason, reached the top at Seven-Mile as he did at the end of *Desert Solitare,* seen the light turn the La Sals crimson and demanded the driver take him back. I understood this. The airline was pulling up stakes, and I had been offered a good airline job in Sun Valley, Idaho, but I too, never wanted to leave.

Years later, I got to meet Edward Abbey a number of times. We had many mutual friends, and he was always very complimentary and encouraging about my work. He was a charming, funny, and kind person, but uncompromising in his principles. Toward the end of his life, he stayed at my house once before he began a long, lazy, late-season river trip through Canyonlands National Park with one of my closest friends. I left my copy of *Slickrock* for him to sign, and he kindly complied. The book is one of my most prized possessions.

I've often said that *Desert Solitaire* should be required reading for anyone crossing the Colorado River bridge into Moab. Having lived my entire adult life in the Moab Valley, I appreciate the achievement of that great book now more than ever. It is chock full of utter truth. What Ed says at the end of his book is true for this book too: "Do not jump into your automobile next June and rush out to the Canyon country hoping to see some of what I have attempted to evoke in these pages.... This is not a travel guide but an elegy. A memorial. You're holding a tombstone in your hands...."

PLATE 13

Balanced Rock and Sunset Clouds
Arches National Park

PLATE 14

The Chocolate Drops
Canyonlands National Park

....

PLATE 15

Hisatsenom (Ancestral Puebloan) Ruin

PLATE 18

Balanced Rock
Arches National Park

··

PLATE 19

Rime Ice on Yucca Spikes
Proposed BLM Wilderness

PLATE 20

North Window with Rainbow
Arches National Park

PLATE 21

Fog
Arches National Park

PLATE 24

Courthouse Towers and Pool
Arches National Park

....

PLATE 25

Snow Covered Fins
Proposed BLM Wilderness

PLATE 27

Rainbow at Delicate Arch
Arches National Park

PLATE 26

Indian Paintbrush and Three Gossips
Arches National Park

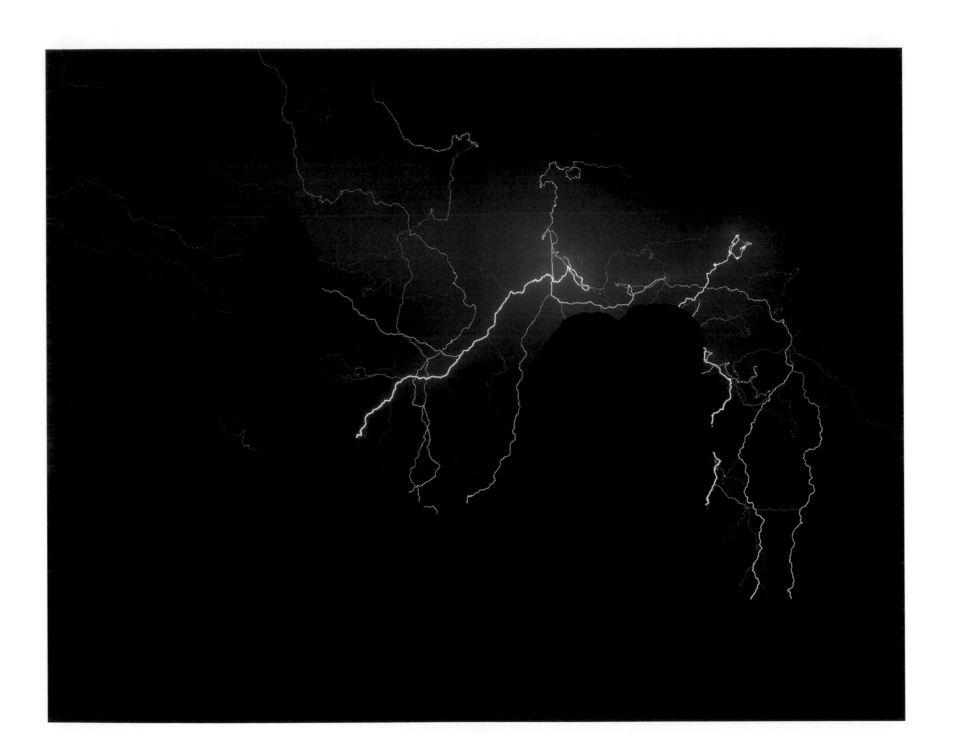

PLATE 33

The Titan
Fisher Towers

PLATE 32

Delicate Arch
Arches National Park

PLATE 36

Walls of Park Avenue
Arches National Park

PLATE 37

Armageddon Rock

PLATE 38

Delta Pool

....

PLATE 39

Castle Rock Rising Above Fog
Proposed BLM Wilderness

PLATE 42

Arch Framing Courthouse Towers
Arches National Park

....

PLATE 43

Turret Arch Seen Through North Window
Arches National Park

CANYONS

PLATE 44

Slot Canyon Waterfall
Proposed BLM Wilderness

Red Queen

A FRIEND introduced me to Claret Cup Canyon. Rock musician Sting has sung about Desert Roses, and a country rock band featuring former members of the Byrds was named after the mythical flower, but there are no "desert roses." Some canyons at higher elevations are adorned with wild roses and others with cliffroses, which are beautiful and aromatic certainly, but they're not crooning material. I think the real desert rose is the cactus flower, and the most stunning cactus flowers of all come with the fully-decked out, screaming eye candy of the claret cup.

Some people could knock around the Canyon Country for years, and never see one, but an *Echinocereus triglochidiatus* in full bloom is equal to a garden of azaleas in a South Carolina spring, or a forest of maples at peak in a New Hampshire autumn. While hiking, you might catch the hint of one out of the corner of your eye—shocking in its intensity and the vividness of its colors in a desert of muted and hushed tones. Nature does not produce such extravagant colors in the wild very often. I think of fish in the Great Barrier Reef, or the green of Ireland. A few people, including me, have become connoisseurs of the plants, which for the most part, grow in solitary clumps separated from each other by miles of canyons. We know where many of them are, and revel in their splendor and rarity. At least that's what I thought, until I saw Claret Cup Canyon. That's not its real name of course, but what else could you call the place where hundreds of these cacti, perhaps more than exist in all other locations, turn the desert into a sea of blood red blooms each May?

Claret cup cacti, according to my friend David Williams' book *A Naturalist's Guide to Canyon Country*, are unusual in a couple of respects. Instead of being pollinated by insects like most cactus, the claret cup procreates with the help of hummingbirds, a fact I can attest to, having seen ruby-throated hummingbirds dive into the scarlet blossoms on several occasions. Many Moab residents have hummingbird feeders to watch the antics of these tiny dynamos, and once, after one had been stunned by a crash into my picture window, I nestled it in my palm for closer inspection as it regained its senses. The stripe on its throat was not red, but a rich royal purple, reminding me of the color of religious vestments I'd seen in my youth. The violet was iridescent in an almost manmade way. The beating heart of the miniature creature was violent in its intensity, shaking the entire body in a pace that would put a head-banging heavy metal fan to shame. In a moment its eyes cleared and it launched from my hand in a twisting course back to the desert. Knowing that these lovely birds were involved in the claret cup life cycle made me love the plant even more.

In late April, I begin a systematic observation of the many subjects in the Canyon. No two are the same. Each has its own personality, so much so, that I begin to think of names for them: Big Red, Crimson Tide, Better Red Than Dead, Red Planet, Red Rain, Bloody Mary, Strawberry Fields Forever. The epithets help me keep track of the progress of each—one may have no buds at

> Nature does not produce such extravagant colors very often...

all while its nearest neighbor shows off with forty. The plants seem to follow their own inner clocks, blooming when they please, with some coming early and others late. Giant mounds of plants, defying expectations, may bring forth only two blossoms, while pedestrian mid-size plants burst forth in abundance. My friend has two neighboring cacti he calls "Vivid" and "Subtle." Though only feet apart, Vivid has the most passionately red blossoms in the canyon, while Subtle's hues are yellowish orange instead of red.

This year, as in last, one cactus near a nondescript rock wall is the most profligate. First, 12 buds appear, in two days there are 30, shortly thereafter the number nearly doubles, but by then some of the first are already beginning to fade. Nearby, an older plant (at least I think it's older because of its world weary look), struggles to produce a meager few blossoms.

I look forward to spring and the ritual of viewing these great wildflower displays. Nature tries to get our attention in so many ways, and occasionally it gets right in our face with beauty so true and vibrant it cannot be denied. I will make a ritual every year of checking every tiny nook of Claret Cup Canyon for more red bouquets. The tiny flame in the rocks is like a voice crying in the wilderness—look here, beneath your feet.

PLATE 48

Slot Canyon
Proposed BLM Wilderness

....

PLATE 47

Green River Overlook

PLATE 53

Waterfall Framed by Cave
Proposed BLM Wilderness

....

PLATE 54

Angel Arch
Canyonlands National Park

PLATE 56

The Confluence
Canyonlands National Park

PLATE 55

Morning Light Streamers
Canyonlands National Park

PLATE 59

Sand and Snow Patterns
Proposed BLM Wilderness Area

....

PLATE 60

Triplet Falls

MOUNTAINS

PLATE 63

Johnson's Up-On-Top

Mr. Till Goes to Washington

A FEW YEARS AGO I was asked by the Southern Utah Wilderness Alliance to testify before a congressional committee. Since I'll try anything once just for the experience—including swimming the holes in Crystal Rapid, driving in Athens, being struck by lightning in my own house, and having spinal taps—I said yes.

The committee in question was investigating the creation of Grand Staircase/Escalante National Monument, an ongoing saga beyond the scope of this book. What is germane about my trip is my Alice-in-Wonderland, mind-bending trip to the halls where land policy for southern Utah and the Moab area is made. I was to testify in favor of the Monument, which I strongly favored and still favor. The great-grandson of Theodore Roosevelt, whose father made the first use of the Antiquities Act, the law President Clinton invoked to create the Monument, as well as Mark Austin, owner of the Boulder Mountain Lodge near the Escalante River in Boulder, Utah also testified in favor of the new Monument. Bruce Babbitt, then Secretary of the Interior, represented the Clinton Administration.

Lined up against us to delineate the evils of the protective measure was every politician in Utah, from county officials from Escalante and Kanab to the dapper Senator Orrin Hatch. Utah Congressman Jim Hansen was in charge of the proceedings, and he had planned a long day of rebukes for those of us in the hot seat with fond feelings for "rocks and stickers." While these attacks continued, I was struck by some of the ironies of the proceedings. Our opponents, who were supposed to hate government and love the private sector, treated the Southern Utah government officials with a kindness and deference bordering on worship. The County Comissioners and other public officials speaking against the Monument were told to keep up the good work, while those of us in favor of the new park were treated with civilized disdain.

Congressman Duncan from Tennessee referred to us as "leftist...socialist...radicals." Ironcially, the entrepreneurial three of us, a stockbroker, a hotel owner and a freelance artist, were probably the only people employed in the private sector in the room. The Congressman further worried that Grand Staircase/Escalante would be overrun with "people who live in big cities and drive their Range Rovers and put on the their L.L. Bean clothing and think of themselves as big outdoorsmen." He also expressed concern (again this was a Newt Gingrich Republican) that these "environmental extremists are almost always real wealthy."

Besides our purity as captalists, Mark, Ted and I paid our travel expenses, while taxpayers funded the Capitol junket of our adversaries. Also, a constant argument made by Hansen and others was that Monument designation would cause overcrowding and overdevelopment in this pristine area. I was actually moved by the un-Reaganesque argument, but a year or so after this hearing, Utah newspapers reported people in Escalante were angry that not enough people had been coming to their outback, and that Grand Staircase/Escalante National Monument was

I'll try anything once just for the experience...

not living up to expectations. The proposed solution? More development.

Strangely enough, my Congressman, Congressman Cannon, did not want to question me much about my five minute statement, instead he wanted to quibble about a word I used.

MR. CANNON: Mr. Till...In the first place, you used the word "icon" which is sort of an odd term. It often suggests a religious devotion. When you used that for these areas down there, did you have any sense of that or did you just mean a beautiful area?

MR. TILL: I guess I don't quite understand your question. I was using "icon" in terms of maybe not the religious connotation, but as something that is set up as a symbol of great beauty, and I think this park will be in the same league as Grand Canyon, or Glacier Bay [both parks created by the same law as Grand-Staircase/Escalante and both parks whose designations were controversial and strongly opposed] in the public perception in the future. That is all I was trying to say.

In his short speech right after mine, Theodore Roosevelt IV explained eloquently why people of all political stripes look to the Congress and the President to protect singular wild landscapes and cultural treasures. He said, "The American people have appreciated the fact that the Federal Government has a legal tool with which to respond to public concerns about the preservation of places that are keystones to our national memory and help define us as a nation and as a people." Mr. Roosevelt could just as well have been speaking about the areas pictured in this book that are still beyond the protection of wilderness designation.

After the sound and fury of the hearings, nothing much has changed. Although Congressmen Hansen and Cannon still tour Southwestern Utah talking about trimming the size of Grand Staircase/Escalante National Monument, the area has been so ingrained on the national consciousness, in part through my photographs, that political support for their schemes could probably never develop. After a place has been celebrated in the pages of *Smithsonian Magazine,* it is hard to erase it from the collective memory or pass it off as something we can easily part with. It has always been my objective to work for the same goal closer to my home, in the land of Moab. The great Southwestern writer John Nichols has said that implicit in every good landscape photograph is the bulldozer just outside the frame. I hope all my imagery, and especially the photographs in this book, are seen in that light.

PLATE 64

Bee Flowers in Spanish Valley

PLATE 65

Ice Encrusted Forest
Manti-La Sal National Forest

PLATE 66

Mountain Shadow
La Sal Mountains

Crossing
to Jordan

Though Moab, Utah may not be named after the biblical desert land, descriptions in the Old Testament of a fiery red isolated desert country seem to fit exactly. I've been to other desert towns that look a lot like the American Moab—Alice Springs, Australia, with its flat-roofed, swamp-cooler-topped homes and encircling cliffs, and San Pedro de Atacama, in Chile, which even has the nearby Sierra La Sal Mountains.

But the land of Moab in Jordan truly bears a striking resemblance to the Utah Moab. There are natural stone arches, petroglyphs, black varnished sandstone cliffs, and ruins of lost civilizations. Even the Bedouin weavings look remarkably like Navajo designs.

Why travel halfway around the world to come home? It could be I'm hoping the proverb is true and that at the end of all my exploring I'll return home to really know that place for the first time.

MOAB
Jordan

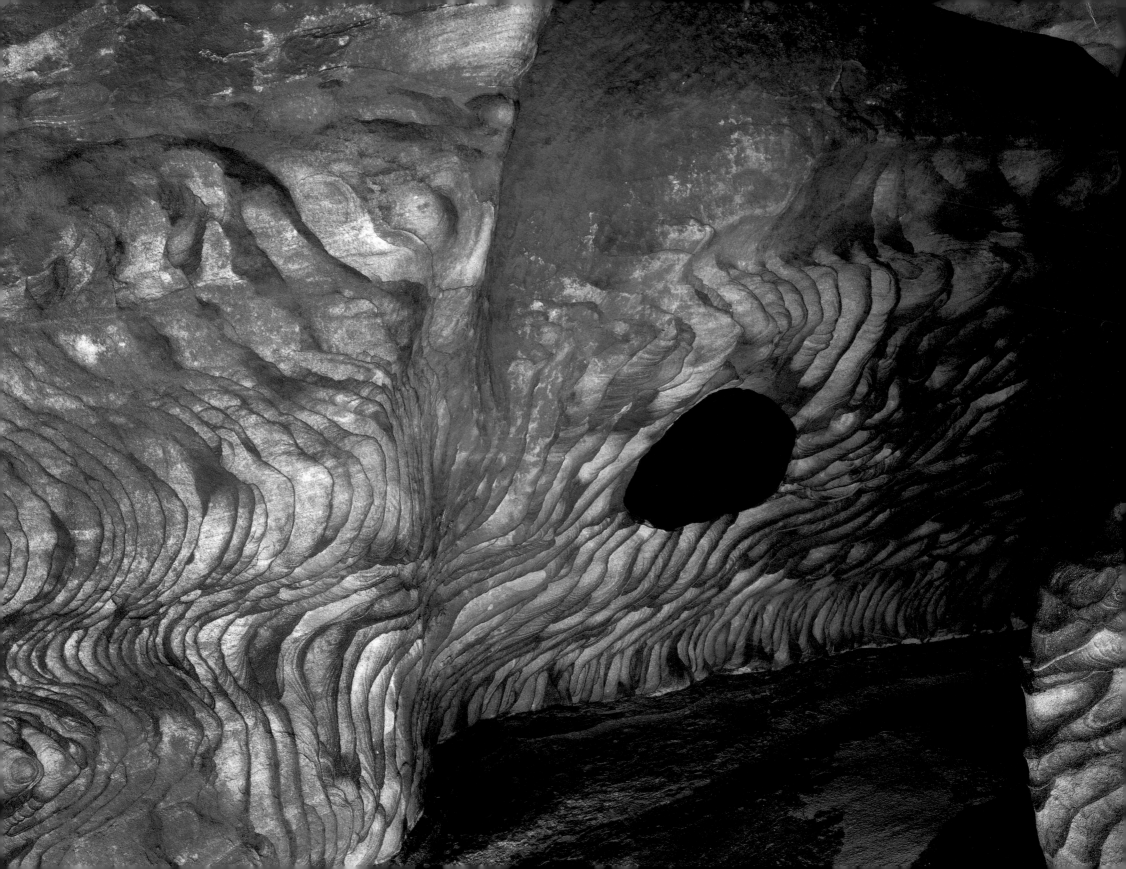

PLATE 77

Nubian Sandstone
Moab, Petra, Jordan

....

PLATE 78

Petra
Moab, Jordan

PLATE INFORMATION

COVER: La Sal Mountains.
Pentax 6x7 90mm lens. Fuji RMS 1/1000 2.8 shot at ISO 1000.

FRONTISPIECE: Moab Valley.
Toyo Field Camera 360mm lens. Velvia f45 1/2.

RIVERS

PLATE 1: S Curve.
Pentax 6x7 with 90mm lens. Kodak VS Film. 5.6/1000.
An aerial photograph, made, as always, with the window of the airplane wide open.

PLATE 2: Pictographs.
Toyo Field Camera with 210mm Rodenstock Apo Sironar lens. Tiffen 812 Filter. Velvia f22 2 seconds.
Lining up the plane of the lens on the view camera with the relatively flat wall helped ensure maximum depth of field.

PLATE 3: Orange River.
Toyo Field Camera with 120mm Schneider lens. Polarizing filter. Velvia f32 1/2.
At times, with flood runoff from very red soils, the Colorado River turns a neon orange. A polarizing filter helped eliminate reflective sheen from the water to saturate the pure color of the water.

PLATE 4: The Diving Board.
Toyo Field Camera with 210mm Rodenstock. Lee 3 stop GND. Velvia f32 8 seconds.
A graduated neutral density filter helped preserve the sunset glow and the deep shadows of the canyon at the same time.

PLATE 5: Iced Grasses.
Toyo Field Camera with 120 Schneider lens. Velvia f45 1/4.

PLATE 6: Fisher Towers, Colorado River.
Toyo Field Camera 600mm Fujinon lens. Velvia f45 4 seconds. Lee 3 stop GND.
The 600mm lens on a 4x5 camera is equal to only about 150mm on a 35mm, but it requires the bellows to be extended about two feet.

PLATE 7: Dead Horse Point.
Toyo Field Camera 120mm Schneider Lens. Polarizing filter. Velvia f22 1 second.
The classic view of Dead Horse Point occurs in the morning hours.

PLATE 8: Green River Reflections.
Toyo Field Camera 180mm Rodenstock lens. Lee 3 stop GND. Velvia f32 8 seconds.
The river was clear as a trout stream when this image was made, making the deep blue sky reflection particularly intense.

PLATE 9: Cataract Canyon.
Toyo Field Camera 75mm Rodenstock lens. Lee 3 stop GND. Velvia f32 2 seconds.
This is one of those compositions that made itself. All I had to do was set up the camera and it was done in less than a minute.

PLATE 10: Waterfall into Colorado River.
Toyo Field Camera with 90mm Rodenstock lens. Lee 3-stop graduated neutral density filter. Kodak VS Film f32 1 second.
The milky water effect comes from the long exposures needed with a 4x5 view camera.

PLATE 11: Buttermilk Clouds.
Toyo Field Camera 75mm Rodenstock Lens. Lee three-stop GND Velvia f32 2 seconds.
Clouds are a key element in my work, and buttermilk clouds are my favorite clouds. They don't happen very often, and, as with much of my work, luck played a big part in obtaining this image. It's one of my favorites.

MESAS

PLATE 12: Wilson Arch.
Toyo Field Camera 90mm Rodenstock lens. Velvia f45 1 second.

PLATE 13: Balanced Rock.
Toyo Field Camera 120mm Schneider lens. Lee 3 Stop GND. Velvia f32 8 seconds.
This incredible antisunset came out of nowhere. I had actually just gone to Balanced Rock to test a new lens, with no plans to do any serious work. Suddenly the clouds appeared and the wonders began. An image I shot just a few minutes earlier has been widely published, this shot came later as the light left the towers and was shining only on the clouds.

PLATE 14: Chocolate Drops.
Olympus OM-1 50mm lens. Kodachrome 64.
This image from 1979 has not appeared in any of my previous books, but it has sentimental value for me as the first photograph I ever published. I do remember that the image was made at the end of a long flight and I needed a bathroom very badly. The original has been lost and all I have left is a duplicate. I have made several attempts to duplicate the shot, but I have been unable to do so.

PLATE 15: Hisatsenom (Ancestral Puebloan) Ruin.
Toyo Field Camera 75mm Rodenstock Lens f45 1 second.
The 4x5 View Camera allows the photographer to be very close to the subject and still keep it all in focus. My camera lens was less than a foot from the left buttress of this amazing series of natural arches framing an Ancestral Puebloan ruin.

PLATE 16: Colorado River, Canyonlands National Park.
Toyo Field Camera 120mm Schneider lens.

PLATE 17: Rainbow Seen from Junction Butte.
Toyo Field Camera 135mm Schneider lens Ektachrome 64.
I'm sure I made the first ascent of Junction Butte with a view camera, and I was rewarded with this stormlight and rainbow.

PLATE 18: Balanced Rock.
Toyo Field Camera 360 Nikkor-T lens. Velvia f45 1 second.

PLATE 19: Rime Ice on Yucca spikes.
Toyo Field Camera 210mm Rodenstock lens. Velvia f45 12 seconds.
Weeks of fog have coated the spikes of this yucca. Although these fog events don't happen often, they can come into the Canyonlands for weeks at a time during the winter.

PLATE 20: North Window.
Toyo Field Camera 180mm Rodenstock lens. Velvia f32 1/2 second.

PLATE 21: Fog in Arches.
Toyo Field Camera 600mm Fujinon lens Velvia f32 1/2 second.
I have seen fog like this in Arches National Park only once in 27 years. Another professional photographer was also at La Sal Mountain Overlook shooting the scene, but she didn't realize how unusual the conditions really were.

PLATE 22: Glory.
Pentax 6x7 90mm lens Velvia 1/1000 f5.6.
Called a glory, or a specter of brocken, this circular fog rainbow appears around the shadow of the viewer, or, in this case, the airplane carrying me and my camera. Early day viewers of the phenomenon thought their own shadow was a spirit being, hence the specter name. I saw three glories in a two year period—this one, one at the Grand Canyon, and one at Machu Picchu. All three were spectacular events.

PLATE 23: Icy Pinyon.
Toyo Field Camera 75mm Nikkor lens. Velvia f32/ 15 seconds.

PLATE 24: Courthouse Towers & Pool.
Toyo Field Camera 90mm Rodenstock lens. Lee 2 stop GND. Velvia f45 1 second.

PLATE 25: Snow-Covered Fins.
Pentax 6x7 90mm lens. Velvia f2.8 1/500.
An aerial view.

PLATE 26: Indian Paintbrush and Three Gossips.
Toyo Field Camera 90mm Rodenstock. Velvia f45 1/2 second. Lee 3 stop GND.
One trick I have is to get the camera right down on the deck. I use a Gitzo Mountaineer tripod with legs that will allow the camera to rest at ground level. A simple tilt with the view camera ensures near/far depth of field.

PLATE 27: Rainbow at Delicate Arch.
Toyo Field Camera 120mm Schneider lens. Velvia f22 15 seconds.
I've hiked to Delicate Arch over 100 times over the years trying to photograph a rainbow with the scenic icon. Finally, in September of 1999, I was lucky enough to have a beautiful rainbow materialize. Unfortunately, a wind-driven rain continued during its short appearance, and I had a lot of rain on my lens when I made the exposure. Consequently, the photo is a little soft and has some haloing from the many raindrops on the surface of the lens.

PLATE 28: Lightning Over Balanced Rock (Clay Schwarck). *Horseman Field Camera 120mm Schneider lens. Velvia f32 30 minutes.*

PLATE 29: Cracked Earth.
Toyo Field Camera 210mm Rodenstock lens. Velvia f45 2 seconds.
This image is a very popular seller at the Tom Till Gallery. Neve Campbell even owns one. It was made as an after thought. I had been photographing a huge field of bee plants when I looked at the cracked earth and flowers just beneath my feet. Although I think the photograph is a good image, I could never have predicted its popularity. I wish I had about 100 more like it.

PLATE 30: Desert Waterfall.
Toyo Field Camera 75mm Rodenstock lens. Lee 3 stop GND. Velvia f 32 2 seconds.

PLATE 31: Spire at Sunrise.
Toyo Field Camera 90mm Rodenstock lens. Lee 3 stop GND. Velvia f22 4 seconds.
It may be apparent that graduated neutral density filters are a big part of my bag of tricks. To the uninitiated, it must be pointed out that these filters have no coloration, and are simply a tool to make the film see more like the eye does. I almost always use the soft variety.

PLATE 32: Delicate Arch Aerial View.
Olympus OM-1 50mm lens. Kodachrome 64 f1.4 1/1,000.
Though the vast majority of the images in this book are from 2000 and 2001, I did dig out a couple of old images that I liked, and which had a very limited publishing history. This is one.

PLATE 33: The Titan.
Pentax 6x7 90mm lens f2.8 1/1,000.
A different view of the big guy in Fisher Towers.

PLATE 34: Rainbow at Wilson Arch.
Toyo Field Camera 75mm Rodenstock lens. Velvia f22 1 second.
This image is also a little soft because of water on the lens. Even with an umbrella, rainbow shooting sometimes requires getting the equipment very wet.

PLATE 35: Dead Horse Point.
Toyo Field Camera 120mm Schneider lens. Velvia f22 1/2 . Lee 3 stop GND filter.
The cloud was so white that I had to use a grad filter to bust it down to the level of the sunlit landscape.

PLATE 36: Walls of Park Avenue.
Toyo Field Camera 360mm Nikkor-T. Velvia f32 1/2.

PLATE 37: Armageddon Rock.
Toyo Field Camera 75mm Rodenstock lens. Velvia f32 1 second.
Sometimes I get to name things I discover and photograph. The names aren't official, but once in a while they stick.

PLATE 38: Delta Pool.
Toyo Field Camera 120mm Schneider lens. Lee 3 stop GND. Velvia f45 1 second.
The scale on this image is somewhat deceiving. The pool is about fifty feet on each side.

PLATE 39: Castle Rock Rising Above Fog.
Toyo Field Camera 360mm Nikkor-T. Velvia f22 1/2 second.
When I arrived at this location a few hours before sunset, the fog appeared much as it does in the final image. Shortly after, the vapors closed in and I was about to give up hope, when, at sunset, Castle Rock appeared again and the fog dropped down below the pinnacles. I'm continually amazed at how often the natural world cooperates with my photographic desires.

PLATE 40: Mesa Arch.
Toyo Field Camera 75mm Rodenstock lens. Velvia f32 4 seconds.

PLATE 41: Frozen Potholes.
Toyo Field Camera 75mm Super Angulon. Ektachrome 64 f32 1/2 second.

PLATE 42: Arch Framing Courthouse Towers.
Toyo Field Camera 75mm Rodenstock lens. Velvia f45 second.
I had scouted the view from this arch six months before I did the photograph. Since the arch faces north I waited until midsummer to go back.

PLATE 43: Turret Arch Seen Through North Window.
Toyo Field Camera 210mm Rodenstock lens. Velvia f45 1 second.
I wanted to improve on this famous view of the two arches, so I waited until I had some great morning clouds to fill the opening. Fortunately, two German tourists kindly moved for a moment while I made the exposure.

CANYONS

PLATE 44: Slot Canyon Waterfall.
Toyo Field Camera 210mm Rodenstock Lens. Velvia f32 2 seconds.
Warm bounce light from slot canyon walls illuminates this waterfall image.

PLATE 45: Claret Cup Cactus.
Toyo Field Camera 210mm Rodenstock Lens. Tiffen 812 filter. Velvia 45 8 seconds.
A Tiffen warming filter was used to counteract the intense blue of the open shade lighting conditions.

PLATE 46: Mossy Stones and Reflections.
Toyo Field Camera 210 Rodenstock lens. Velvia f45 8 seconds.
Under the loupe there are worlds within worlds in this image. I may consider doing a book on just this picture, with tiny pieces blown large. Just kidding.

PLATE 47: Green River Overlook.
Toyo Field Camera 210mm Rodenstock lens. Velvia f22 2 seconds.

PLATE 48: Slot Canyon.
Toyo Field Camera 120mm Schneider lens. Velvia f32 8 seconds.

PLATE 49: Whipple's Fishhook Cactus.
Toyo Field Camera 210mm Schneider lens. Velvia f64 15 seconds.

PLATE 50: Hovenweep Moon Set.
Pentax 6x7 600mm lens. Kodak VS. f8 1 second.
Since long telephotos are impractical with a 4x5, I often use a Pentax 6x7 or a Nikon for distant subjects. Most of my moonrise images are planned out. I pick a subject that will work with a large moon (usually shot on the night before full moon) and use the shadows of trees to point just to the right of where the moon will rise.

PLATE 51: Castle Rock.
Pentax 6x7 600mm lens Kodak VS. f8 1/15 second.

PLATE 52: Waterfall over Schist.
Toyo Field Camera 90mm Super Angulon. Ektachrome 64 f32 1 second.
An older image of a rare snow melt waterfall in Westwater Canyon, this picture was made on the morning of a very bad weather day. I was rowing my own boat through the canyon in February and ran into a blizzard later in the afternoon.

PLATE 53: Waterfall Framed by Cave.
Toyo Field Camera 75mm Rodenstock lens.
Velvia f32 2 seconds.
The ephemeral waterfalls of canyon country are something to behold. I never tire of viewing them and trying to capture their beauty on film.

PLATE 54: Angel Arch.
Toyo Field Camera 210mm Rodenstock lens.
Fujichrome 100 f32 1/4 second.

PLATE 55: Morning Light Streamers.
Toyo Field Camera 360mm Nikkor-T lens.
Velvia f32 2 seconds.
In trying to do something different than the standard shot at Mesa Arch, I was rewarded with a stormy morning and a weird purple/brown colorcast.

PLATE 56: The Confluence.
Toyo Field Camera 120mm Schneider.
Velvia f22/ 1/8.

PLATE 57: Cottonwood Leaves in Stream.
Toyo Field Camera 90mm Rodenstock Velvia
f32 1 second.
Most people don't realize that a reflection is focused at infinity, making full depth of field on this image difficult to obtain without the tilts of a large format camera.

PLATE 58: Columbine and Greenery at a Spring.
Toyo Field Camera 90mm Rodenstock Velvia
f45 2 seconds.

PLATE 59: Sand and Snow.
Toyo Field Camera 180mm Rodenstock lens.
Velvia f45 4 seconds.

PLATE 60: Triplet Falls.
Toyo Field Camera 180mm Rodenstock lens
Velvia f32 1 second.

PLATE 61: Sandstone Cave.
Toyo Field Camera 75mm Rodenstock lens.
Velvia f32 4 seconds.
Light only enters the bottom of this huge sandstone cave (one of the world's largest) during the winter solstice period. Many of my photographs, like this one, can only be done at favorable times of the year, and most require frequent return visits to capture the subject at just the "light" moment.

PAGE 62: Pinyon Nuts, Lichen and Rock.
Toyo Field Camera 210 Rodenstock lens. Velvia
f45 3 seconds.
While being filmed for a television article, I took this abstract image just to give the cameraman footage of me working in the field. I was surprised that I really liked the photograph later on. These surprises help keep photography interesting and fresh for me. Although I can previsualize and predict my results most of the time, at other times they still keep me guessing.

MOUNTAINS

PLATE 63: Johnson's Up On-Top.
Toyo Field Camera 360mm Nikkor-T Velvia
f32 1 second.

PLATE 64: Bee Flowers in Spanish Valley.
Toyo Field Camera 90mm Nikkor.
Ektachrome 64 f32 1/2 second.
The field of flowers was a result of a very hard, wet winter and a rainy spring. Unfortunately, the field is now a borrow pit.

PLATE 65: Ice-Encrusted Forest.
Toyo Field Camera Rodenstock 75mm lens.
Velvia f45 1 second.

PLATE 66: Mountain Shadows.
Pentax 6x7 90mm lens. Kodak VS f2.8 1/500.

PLATE 67: Rare Red Aspens.
Toyo Field Camera 360mm Nikkor-T. Velvia
f45 1/2 second.
Some pockets of red aspens occur from time to time in Southern Utah mountains, providing splendid photo subjects.

PLATE 68: Giant Paintbrush.
Toyo Field Camera 120mm Schneider lens.
Velvia f45 1 second.
I noticed this amazing paintbrush plant and returned to try make the photograph at dawn the next day. That morning was cloudy and very windy, so I came back a third time the following day when, fortunately, calm conditions prevailed.

PLATE 69: La Sal Mountain Reflection.
Toyo Field Camera 360 Nikkor-T lens. Velvia
f45 4 seconds. Lee 3 stop GND filter.

PLATE 70: Sunset over Moab Valley.
Toyo Field Camera 360mm Nikkor -T-lens.
Fujichrome 100 f45 1/2.
The air in the Canyon Country is so dry that shooting the orb of the sun at sunset or sunrise is very difficult. This storm allowed me to do so by filtering the sun's ray through a sunset wall of rain.

PLATE 71: Reeds in Shallow Lake.
Toyo Field Camera 135mm Schneider lens.
Ektachrome 64 f32/ 1/8.

PLATE 72: Aspen Leaves and Falls.
135mm Schneider lens. Ektachrome 64
f32 1 second.

PLATE 73: Aspen Trees in Autumn.
Toyo Field Camera 210mm lens. Velvia
f45 1/2 second.

PLATE 74: Aspens and Oaks.
Toyo Field Camera 360mm Nikkor-T.
Ektachrome 64 f45 1/4 second.

PLATE 75: Icy Aspen Trees.
Toyo Field Camera 360mm Nikkor-T. Velvia
f 45 1 second.

PLATE 76: Cliff Dwelling.
Linhof Master Technica 600mm Fujinon
Lee 3 stop GND Velvia f32 16 seconds.

JORDAN

PLATE 77: Nubian Sandstone.
Toyo Field Camera 210mm Rodenstock lens.
Velvia f45 1/2 second.
An abstract image of the very colorful and interesting Nubian sandstone. The black hole is a tiny cave.

PLATE 78: Petra.
Toyo Field Camera 90mm Rodenstock lens.
Velvia f45 1/2 second.

PLATE 79: Wadi Rum.
Toyo Field Camera 75mm Rodenstock lens.
Lee 3-stop GND. Velvia f45 2 seconds.

PLATE 80: Wadi Rum.
Toyo Field Camera 75mm Rodenstock lens
Polarizing filter. Velvia f45 2 seconds.
The polarizing filter removed sheen from the rock surface, making the petroglyphs more intense.

PHOTOGRAPHY NOTES

I want to thank the many people who have written to me over the course of my career with kind comments. Especially since the advent of email, and the establishment of Tom Till Gallery, the positive response to my work has been a great inspiration to me. Unfortunately, I have begun to get so many letters that sometimes, especially if I'm spending a lot of time in the field, I am unable to respond to all of them. I sincerely apologize.

I enjoy this praise, and my wife is adept at helping me keep my feet on the ground. I probably would have been more successful if I'd adopted the regal bearing that some nature photographers don so convincingly, but I firmly believe that I'm only "a legend in my own lunchtime," as the Irish say. All I've ever wanted to do, really, is make a living from hiking and put my kids through college. I love this country. It's the star of the show, not me, If some of that love shines through to you in the photographs here, I will have succeeded.

OTHER BOOKS BY TOM TILL

Colorado: Images from Above

Outcroppings

Utah: Magnificent Wilderness

Utah Compass Guides

New Jersey: Images of the Landscape

Visions of the Colorado Plateau

American Southwest

Utah: A Centennial Celebration

The Woven Spirit

Visions of the North

Utah Reflections

Utah Wildflowers

Slickrock Country

Iowa: Smithsonian Guides to Natural America

Sacred Images

Always in Season

Colorado Plateau: The Land, The Indians

New Mexico Wilderness

Seasons in the Rockies

Utah: Then and Now

Great Ghost Towns of the West

Along New Mexico's Continental Divide Trail

Continental Divide Trail Guide, New Mexico